Paper Flowers

First published in the United States of America by:
Quarry Books, an imprint of
Rockport Publishers, Inc.
146 Granite Street
Rockport, Massachusetts 01966-1299
Telephone: (508) 546-9590
Fax: (508) 546-7141

Distributed to the book trade and art trade in the United States by:
North Light, an imprint of F & W Publications
1507 Dana Avenue
Cincinnati, Ohio 45207
Telephone: (513) 531-2222

ISBN 1-56496-275-X

10 9 8 7 6 5 4 3 2 1

Designer
Kristen Webster
Blue Sky Limited

Photography
Michael Lafferty
Additional Photography
Douglas Cannon

Manufactured in Hong Kong by Excel Printing

Paper Flowers

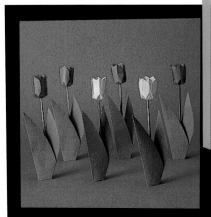

Michael G. LaFosse

QUARRY BOOKS
Rockport, Massachusetts

Contents

Introduction

Flowers and butterflies are splendid subjects to render in paper and their forms are open to wide interpretation. The patterns in this book are designed to take best advantage of the paper provided, but they will work with any papers of similar weight and folding characteristics.

Many methods of paper flower-making require special materials such as crepe paper, wire, florist's tape, and dowels. Not so with these patterns! The simple techniques in this book will produce stunning results with even the most ordinary papers. Experiment with the paper provided, then use the blank tracing patterns in the back of the book to make flowers from any material you choose. Or adapt these flower designs to create dozens of other plants and butterflies of your own. I have used these flower-making techniques for many occasions, from adorning banquet tables to decorating display windows in SAKS Fifth Avenue, New York.

Enjoy!

—Michael G. LaFosse

How to Use This Book

Each flower project begins with a list of materials and a picture of the finished flower. The papers provided are marked with folding lines for your first attempts, and the templates in the back of the book can be traced to make an endless supply of flower patterns. To get the best possible results, the three most important things to keep in mind are: cut slowly and carefully, fold precisely, and get to know the key. The key on page 9 explains the fold lines and arrows (known as the Yoshizawa/Randlet standardized origami system) that accompany each drawing in this book. If you are already familiar with this system of folding notation you will feel right at home; otherwise, spend a few minutes learning to recognize the symbols and to understand the terminology.

Begin by cutting out all paper elements for the desired project from the supply sheets provided at the back of the book. Use sharp, comfortable shears and take your time. A razor-blade tool (such as an X-acto knife) makes clean work of detailed areas. Protect your work surface by placing a piece of cardboard under anything you are cutting with a blade. For most projects in this book you will need a ruler or some other straight-edge, along with a tool to score fold lines on the back of the flower elements.

Study the step-by-step photos carefully, to visually check your work. It is often helpful to look ahead at the next diagram or photo to see the results of a fold in advance. Take time to perform the folds neatly and accurately.

Though adhesives are not always necessary, you may wish to make your creations last longer by adding a little white glue or paste at key contact points. Apply adhesives sparingly and neatly, and have a damp cloth handy to wipe away any spills.

Blue tracing patterns are included for each project, so that you can make additional flowers from whatever materials you choose. The showcase at the end of each project offers variations on each flower, for added inspiration.

Glossary & Key

Because the illustrations can show only a segment of a project's folding procedure, it is helpful to know whether the paper is being folded in front or from behind. The origami system of Valley-folds and Mountain-folds uses two kinds of broken lines (see key diagram) to show when to fold toward the project's surface (valley-fold) and when to fold behind the surface (mountain-fold.)

Valley-fold - Relative to the displayed view of the paper being folded, a valley-fold is always folded in front of the project's surface. If you were to unfold a valley-fold you would see a valley-crease, which dents into the paper's surface forming a valley.

Mountain-fold - Relative to the displayed view of the paper being folded, a mountain-fold is always folded behind the project's surface. If you were to unfold a mountain-fold you would see a mountain-crease, which rises up from the paper's surface forming a mountain ridge.

Various types of arrows help make the folding instructions even clearer. These arrows are easy to understand with a quick study of the illustrated key. Whenever you see the repeat arrow in a diagram, you must apply the demonstrated folding procedure to all indicated parts of the project.

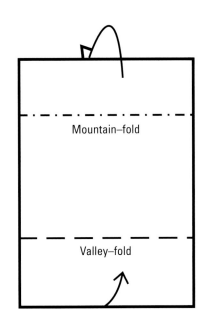

Mountain–fold

Valley–fold

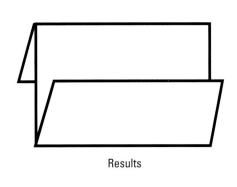

Results

Standard Symbols

Valley-fold

Mountain-fold

Directional Arrows   In Front   Behind

Turn Model Over

Insert/Apply Pressure

Repeat

Enlarged View

Paper Rose

Although they are not as fragrant, paper roses last much longer than the real ones do. Since real roses come in all shapes and sizes, there is a lot of room for creative license when making a paper rose. Shades of red and pink are classic rose colors, but yellow, white, peach, and even near-black garnet, are all shades that can be found in real roses and that can be adopted for a bouquet of the paper variety.

If you like long-stemmed roses, such as tea roses, remember that they can look spindly on their own. Fill in your arrangement with shorter-stemmed primroses, or luxuriously petaled cabbage roses. Since roses have layers of beautifully unfurling petals, you will get the best results if you study a few real roses before attempting this project.

Materials

- *Rose template*

- *Scissors*

- *White glue*

- *Ruler or other straightedge*

- *Scoring tool (such as a letter opener)*

- *Pencil or toothpick (to open a hole in base of blossom)*

How to Build a Rose

The blossom shown here requires only four pieces to complete. You may scale the pattern down to create charming miniature roses, or make the scale larger for a more dramatic display. Adding paper stems and leaves (demonstrated on page 14) will make your flowers even more beautiful and lifelike. The rose pattern can be used as it appears, or adapted to create carnations by using pinking shears to cut the pattern from tissue paper. Double or triple the tissue for each layer of the blossom pattern, to provide extra petals and more support for the flower, then fluff open the layers after assembly.

Colorful fabrics make wonderful roses, too: if you lightly coat the back of the selected fabric with spray adhesive and apply a thin paper backing, the rose pattern will look like fabric and fold like paper. Use these fabric roses as coordinated interior accents.

Once you have mastered the folded rose by using the special pattern at the end of the book, try experimenting with other paper textures, colors, and patterns. This simple method produces stunning results from even the most ordinary paper. Try newspapers, magazine pages, or book covers; or use coupons, concert tickets, or seed packets—the list is endless. After a time, you may find yourself going beyond the scope of this book and applying the rose technique to create dozens of other plant and butterfly designs.

Rose Tips

- *Once all of the elements are cut out, clean the work area of any scraps of paper or debris that could later be confused with the actual flower cutouts.*
- *For maximum "grab", make only a small hole in the bottom of each part of the blossom, then let the paper stem enlarge the hole by itself.*
- *The leaves may be arranged any way that you feel looks best. Try making additional pockets and leaves, or skip the pockets altogether and glue the leaves to the outside of the stem.*
- *You may choose to glue the stem closed once the blossom is inserted. Blossoms and leaves can also be used alone, without a stem.*

1 Following the fold-lines, score the backs of petals using a letter opener and straightedge. Turn the paper over.

2 Make pleats, starting on the left side of the petal and working left to right. The score lines will guide you. Fold loosely at first, then tighten the entire piece to finish.

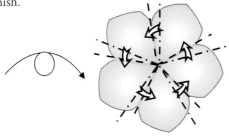

3 Fold each petal down, to make the shape pictured here. This fold extends only halfway across each petal. You may also curl the petals, for a softer effect.

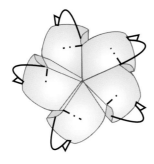

4 Pierce a small hole in the center of each unit (a sharp pencil works well for this); keep the hole as small as possible.

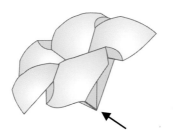

5 Make the center spike by repeatedly folding triangle in half (a-c). Be sure that your folds are tight and sharp. Curl the flag tightly around top of spike and make a cone shape (d & e). You may loosen this curled paper after the blossom has been assembled.

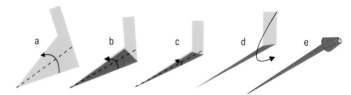

6 Assemble blossom. You may apply a small amount of glue where the petals meet the spike (optional, but recommended for permanent displays.) White glue works best.

optional glue points

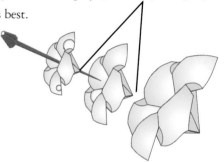

7 Fold each leaf in half, lengthwise. Make an angled crease as a guide. The angled crease sets the direction and spread for veins in the leaves. Make all creases sharp.

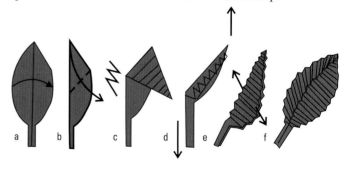

8 Next, tightly fan-fold the leaves. You may vary the width of each pleat, narrower toward the tip and wider at the center. Open out each leaf completely and shape it with your fingers. If you want to add a stem, follow the folding method shown in the line drawings below.

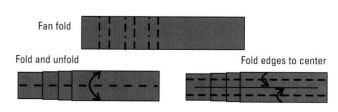

Fan fold

Fold and unfold

Fold edges to center

9 Insert leaves into stem. Be sure that you insert the leaves on the smooth, outside of the stem (side with no raw edges showing). Pay close attention to which side of each leaf is uppermost. Glue is not necessary here.

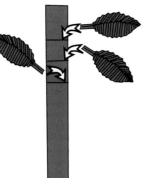

10 Fold the stem in half (lengthwise) once again, on the existing center-fold line. Hide the raw edges inside and narrow the stem.

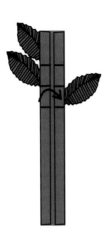

11 Finally, insert the blossom into the top end of the finished stem. Choose a secure group of layers to do this. You may apply a small amount of white glue for permanence.

12 Perfect roses—ready for display.

Rose Shortcuts

You can skip the pocket folds when making the stems. Glue the leaves directly to the outside surface of the finished stem. Use only two petal segments for each flower; the top two together will make a small blossom, the bottom two—a larger blossom. Single petal segments (alone) make pretty apple or cherry blossoms.

Rose Gallery

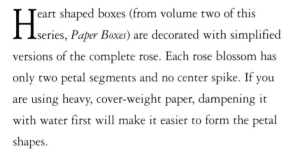

Heart shaped boxes (from volume two of this series, *Paper Boxes*) are decorated with simplified versions of the complete rose. Each rose blossom has only two petal segments and no center spike. If you are using heavy, cover-weight paper, dampening it with water first will make it easier to form the petal shapes.

Richly colored and velvety, handmade oriental papers make these roses look real. Oriental papers are strong but soft in texture. Make them easier to work with by pasting two sheets together, as suggested for newspaper.

Decorate a cake. Plastic-coated decorative foils come in many colors, and are excellent for making flowers and leaves. Prevent grease stains by placing small pieces of wax paper between flowers and frosting. Use only food-grade materials on edible cakes.

Rose brooch with green and gold foil leaves. Brooch pins may be purchased as blanks (check local craft stores). Assemble the floral decoration, then attach it to the pin with hot-melt glue.

Newspapers, or printed pages from any source, are great for making flowers. Prepare magazine or newsprint papers by pasting together two layers for a thicker, more durable sheet; then cut out pattern pieces and follow the steps. Very effective in advertising and for point-of-sale displays.

Paper Tulip

There are more than three thousand—and counting—varieties of tulips. This makes life easy for the would-be paper tulip maker. Choosing paper colors for these flowers is simple: almost anything goes. The stems are a different story, since tulips bloom early in the spring their paper counterparts should have pale-green paper stems.

A newly popular tulip variety, the Parrot tulip, has bright, striped and fringed petals that are worth trying to recreate in paper. The trick for making *any* variety of tulip in paper is keeping the shapes of the flowers from being too uniform. Copy real tulips and make each paper bloom with a slight imperfection, a few odd-size petals, petals that are tightly shut, or slightly shallow and open petals. Varying the size and form of paper tulips takes away the stiffness their cupped shape is prone to, and makes them seem airy and light.

Materials

- *Tulip template*

- *Scissors*

- *White glue*

- *Ruler or other straightedge*

- *Scoring tool (such as a letter opener)*

- *Pencil or toothpick (to open a hole in base of blossom)*

How to Build a Tulip

Fields of colorful tulips are easy to make with our method. Use any type of brightly colored paper. Once mastered, this paper tulip will surely become your favorite. You will be surprised at how easily they can be made, and at how life-like they look.

These tulips are especially good for table-top and window displays, since they stand up very well on their own. Like the paper rose, tulips can easily be scaled up or down—to create miniature or life-size collections. Tiny tulip plants, two- to five-inches high, make wonderful lapel pins and package ornaments. Include a few life-size paper tulips in spring cut-flower arrangements; they will add drama and color without being overpowering.

Feel free to experiment with the final shapes of the petals and leaves; adding a curl here and there or possibly changing the outlines as you cut out the paper patterns. Photographs of real tulips in garden catalogs and books are great for inspiration: so are visits to gardens and nursery centers, where you can gather ideas about color combinations and display. Above all, let the qualities of the materials speak out— good paper always has something worthwhile to say.

Tulip Tips
- *When using the 1/2 leaf pattern, first fold the paper in half and align the short edge of the pattern shape to the folded edge of the paper. Cut out the shape and you will have the first fold of the leaf set already done.*
- *Make longer stems from heavy paper for arrangements with cut flowers in containers. Glue the blossoms in place for permanence.*
- *For a more interesting and dramatic tulip, use spray cement to glue contrasting colors of thin papers back-to-back. Cut and fold the blossom from this paper as usual. The center of the finished tulip will be a different color than the petals.*
- *Bright, solid colors work best for most tulips, but include some variegated colors in large displays. Vary the hue of the green stems and leaves in large displays, to add depth. In any arrangement, make some blossoms more open than others. This adds a natural touch.*

1 Following the lines, score the inside (light-colored side) of the petals using a letter opener and straightedge. Do not press so hard that you tear the paper.

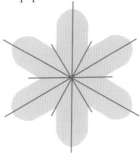

2 Select any petal and fold it upward to its opposite partner, matching the V-notches (on either side of the petal) to the horizontal center line.

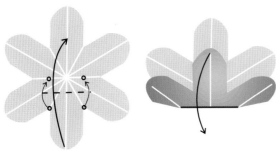

3 Open up the folded paper. The blue line in the illustration for Step Two indicates the crease you have just made. Repeat steps Two and Three for the remaining five petals. For more control, rotate the paper as you work, folding each petal away from you—from the bottom to the top.

   Open the paper flat. There will be a six-pointed, star-shaped crease pattern in the center of the flower. Make a small hole in the center of the flower, using a sharp pencil or other such tool. Turn the paper over.

Study the folding pattern. You will be mountain-folding the outline of the hexagon in the center of the paper, you will also be mountain-folding the short lines from the corners of the hexagon to the V-notches. The valley-fold lines are created by folding the outside edges of every other petal to the center line of that petal. The result will be a cup-shaped tulip blossom with overlapping petals, three on the inside and three on the outside.

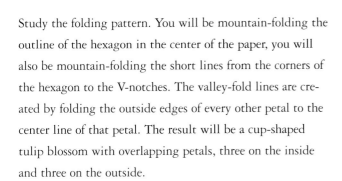

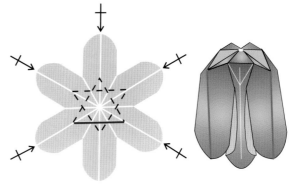

4 Observe the diamond-shaped creases on the bottom out-side of the blossom (there are six). With a little pressure from your finger, dent in the three diamonds that belong to the three outside petals. This will give the bottom of the blossom a pleasing, rounded shape.

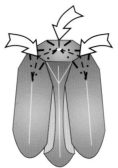

5 Fold the stem as follows: Crease in a center line, then fold the outside edges to this center line. Finally, fold in half again, lengthwise.

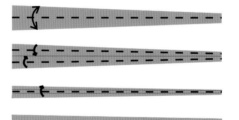

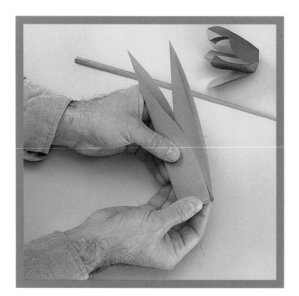

6 Prepare a leaf base by folding the leaf paper in half, tip to tip (a). Fold in half the long way, curved edges together (b). Grasp the inner point and swivel it out, allowing the base line to change position (c). Fold the bottom corners of the leaf section inside. This secures the shape and adds a more dynamic stance (d). The leaf set should stand on its own (e).

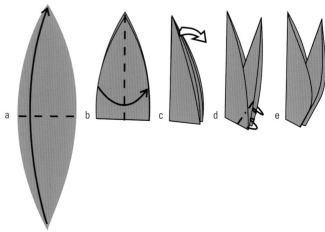

7 Fit the wide end of the stem into the base (glue is optional) and insert the narrow end of the stem into the hole in the bottom of the tulip. Slide the tulip blossom down the stem until it is well seated. Cut off any excess stem.

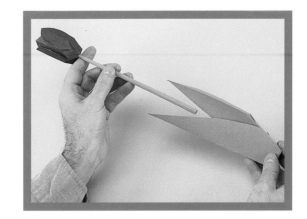

8 The completed tulip—ready for display.

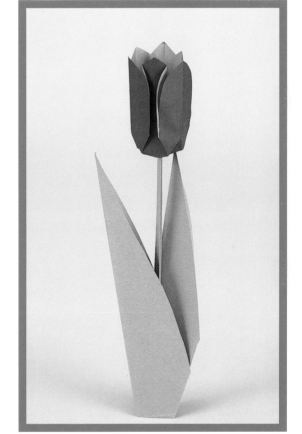

Tulip Shortcuts

Once you are comfortable with the full folding and shaping method of the tulip blossom, you may wish to try a more direct method and save some time. Omit the creasing of the six-pointed star. Go directly to the procedure pictured in the third photo and fold the petal edges parallel to and against the center line of the petals between them. Remember to form a flat base at the bottom center of the blossom.

Tulip Gallery

Only three-inches tall, these tiny tulip plants become charming ornaments with the addition of a loop of thread attached to the top of the stem, inside the blossom.

Long-stem arrangements of tulips and roses. The tulips provide bright colors while the roses fill in the composition. Slender iris leaves add touches of green.

Use a small cluster of tulip blooms as ornaments on a gift package. To add a dramatic contrast of color, insert yellow paper posies in the base of each tulip. For small flowers, reduce and simplify the shapes of the leaves. Papers for these flowers were handmade by the author.

Miniature tulips can also be worn as a smart lapel pin. Glue the tulips to a small clasp pin or attach them directly with a straight pin.

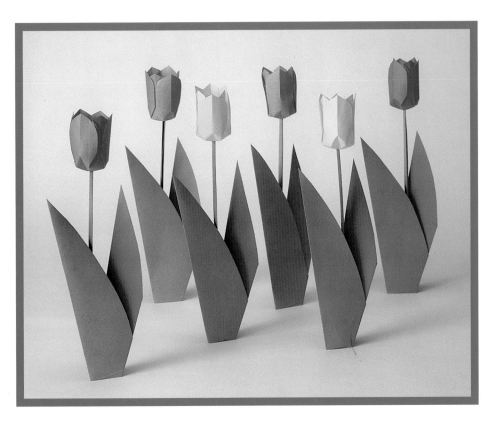

A free-standing tabletop display of paper tulips. The green plant parts for these life-size tulips were created with a heavy, cover-stock paper. Very sturdy and stable, these flowers require no additional support.

Paper Daisy

Whether you think of them as weeds or wildflowers, daisies have been crowding lawns

and filling out bouquets for as long as either was invented. There are daisies to fit every

personality; they can be small, dainty white flowers, or brash, saucer-size Shasta daisies in

neon pink, yellow, and lavender. If you pull apart the blossom of a real daisy, you'll find

the center is made up of many little "flowers" that give it a fuzzy look. Daisies belong to

the same group of flowers as asters, marigolds, goldenrod, and sunflowers—so you can

take color cues from any of these for making paper daisies. Snip paper petals into a tight

fringe to mimic English daisies, or make them smooth and generously overlapping for

Shasta and Michaelmas daisies.

How to Build a Daisy

Daisies come in all colors and sizes. The contrasting color of the center "button" gives these flowers a perky, wide-awake effect. It is no wonder that we equate daisies with a cheerful outlook, and use them for creating "get well" and "congratulations" bouquets for friends and loved ones.

This daisy form is especially suited for arrangements that are wide and shallow, which is the ideal shape for a dining table centerpiece. Coordinate daisy centerpieces to the occasion or season by choosing appropriately colored papers: pastels for a spring bouquet, or golds and russets for an autumn arrangement. You can also coordinate the color of the flowers with the colors of your table setting or room interior.

Daisies are the perfect filler item in floral arrangements, they make a good background for long-stemmed flowers. Short-stemmed daisies are ideal as boutonnieres or package ornaments: if you add longer stems, they work well with slim flowers such as irises and lilies. For a bright accent or pretty garland, string single blossoms together in a classic daisy chain.

Materials

- *Daisy paper elements*

- *Scissors and/or X-acto knife*

- *White glue*

- *Ruler or other straightedge*

- *Scoring tool*

- *Pencil or toothpick (to open a hole in base of blossom)*

- *Toothpick (to wind paper strip for the center)*

Daisy Tips

- *When selecting papers to make daisies, choose colors that match the season or theme. Dark green paper leaves and stems will emphasize the perky effect of the blossoms.*

- *Make longer stems and extra leaves for arrangements of flowers in tall containers, or for mixing with the other paper flowers in this book.*

- *For a faster finish, glue leaves directly to the flower stems. You can also glue the blossoms in place to make the daisy more durable.*

- *If you cut out small blossoms with an X-acto knife the results will be neater and the work will go faster.*

1 Following the fold lines, score the back (light-colored side) of the paper between the petals with a scoring tool and straightedge. Turn the paper over. Score the front (dark-colored side) from tip to tip, across the center line of the petals. Repeat scoring steps on another paper cutout; you will need two for each daisy.

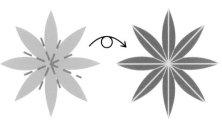

2 Using a pencil or toothpick, pierce a hole in the center of the daisy. Be careful not to make the hole too large—since the paper must be snug enough for the stem to get a good hold.

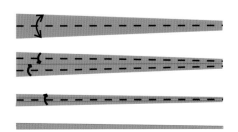

3 Make stems by folding the paper strip in half twice, lengthwise, to get a thin, four-layered paper spear.

4 Glue two yellow strips end-to-end for each daisy center. Wind this strip tightly around a toothpick and glue the outside end to the body of the coil. Carefully remove the toothpick when the glue has dried, thus leaving a hole in the center of the coiled button.

5 Fold the leaves in half lengthwise (a). Make an angled crease as a guide (b). Fan-fold the leaf parallel to the angle guide (c). Open the leaf completely and shape (d-f).

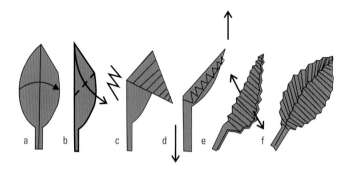

6 To assemble, place one daisy cutout over the other. Take care to stagger the petals so that all sixteen petals are visible. Spear the set of petals and the button-center with the paper stem.

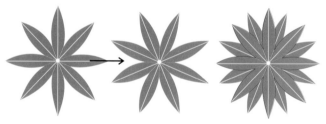

7 Make sure that the stem is snugly in place, then trim any excess paper from the center. You may use glue to make the flower more durable.

8 The finished daisy—ready for display.

Daisy Gallery

Informal arrangements of
daisies bring a touch of
summer to any room.

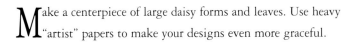

Make a centerpiece of large daisy forms and leaves. Use heavy "artist" papers to make your designs even more graceful.

A classic daisy chain worn as a crown. Glue paper daisies to ribbon, or string them together to create decorative borders, garlands, and wreaths.

In place of a bow, paper daisies are a cheerful surprise as a package ornament. Perfect for decorating a summertime birthday or shower gift.

Paper Iris

Irises are related to lilies, and come in nearly as many shapes, sizes, and colors as do roses. Bearded iris, dwarf iris, Dutch, French, and Japanese irises, each has its own distinct appearance. To recreate irises in paper, use a paper with high rag content for bearded varieties, and a stiff, slightly shiny paper for making the crisp, dwarf varieties of iris. A quick glance at a garden catalog will supply enough color inspiration for a whole field of flowers: bright violet *Ruffled; Breathless,* with flamingo-pink blossoms; *China Maid,* petals in a blend of pink, buff, and lilac; *Crystal,* in bright, frosty blue; or *Frost and Flame,* pure white flowers with tangerine-colored beards.

Of the irises listed, dwarf irises are the easiest to mimic in paper, bearded irises are more difficult, and the Japanese variety is trickiest of all. Japanese irises are wide and flat, but soft in appearance. It takes careful planning to find (or adapt) paper that can be cut to so large a shape without excessive stiffness or without drooping under its own weight.

How to Build an Iris

Materials

- *Iris paper elements*

- *Scissors or X-acto knife*

- *White glue*

- *Ruler or other straightedge*

- *Scoring tool*

Named after Iris, the Greek goddess of the rainbow, this flower was the source of inspiration for the stylized fleur-de-lis design. Large and showy, the iris is an outstanding addition to any garden or flower arrangement, and a must on the list of paper flowers gathered for this collection.

The slim, graceful profile of the iris shows best when displayed as a single stem or in a small grouping of three. If you want to make a larger spray of flowers you will need extra leaves, or some more open paper flower-shapes, to fill out the bouquet.

The iris shown is a simplified rendition, requiring only a single piece of paper for the blossom. Although any color is suitable, remember that the iris is a spring and early summer plant. Paper in hues of pale pink and mauve, deep purple and lavender, or rich tints of yellow will offer the most natural-looking results. Once attached to its stem and leaf, the simple lines of this flower form become quite striking. Just a few of these blooms will add drama to any arrangement.

Iris Tips

- *For best effect, choose two-tone paper with a contrasting hues on either side. Use bright or dusty greens for the stems and leaves.*

- *A round pencil will curl flower petals better than a six-sided one; the facets leave unsightly horizontal rib marks.*

- *As noted before, the blossom is more durable if it is glued to the stem. Try to leave as little stem as possible showing inside the flower.*

- *When using the iris as the only flower in an arrangement, cut stems to varying lengths. Use iris leaves separately and insert into mixed arrangements of paper flowers.*

1 On the outside (light hue side) of the paper, mountain-fold and unfold across gap notches between petals. Repeat with the other two sets of opposing gap notches, folding the shape in half three times in this manner.

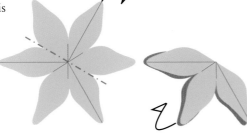

2 Pierce the center to make a small hole for the stem.

3 The blossom papers provided for this project have a line dividing three of the petals in half. I will refer to this as the centerline. Notice also that these three lines are arranged in a symmetrical triangle. On either side of each centerline is a mountain-crease. Fold each mountain-crease against and aligned to its corresponding centerline. Repeat with the other two sets of centerlines and mountain-folds. You will end up with three petals on the outside and three petals on the inside.

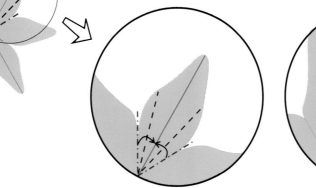

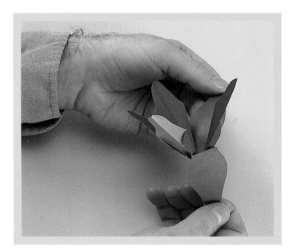

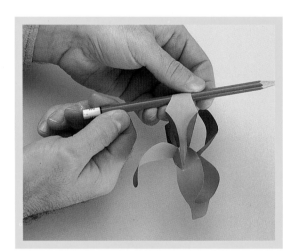

4 Fold down the three outside petals as far as they can go. Make a sharp, horizontal crease at the point where each petal attaches to the flower. Make sure all of the creases made thus far are very crisp.

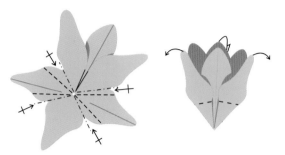

5 If your folding is neat and sharp, you will not need glue to keep the blossom in good form. Give the three outer petals a slight downward curl. Curl the three inner petals toward the center of the flower.

6 Make stems by folding the stem paper in half twice, lengthwise, to get a thin, four-layered paper spear. Two-thirds from the bottom of the leaf, fold the leaf in half lengthwise. You may then leave the leaf straight or gently curl it downward.

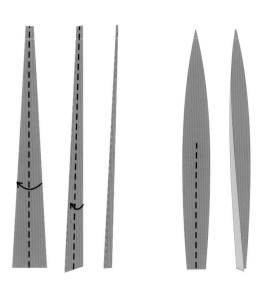

7 Insert the stem through the center hole from the bottom. Glue the leaf to the base of the stem. More than one leaf per stem and flower is a nice touch. You may also use iris leaves by themselves, to add green to other arrangements. Make extra leaves so that you can adjust the final composition of your flowers.

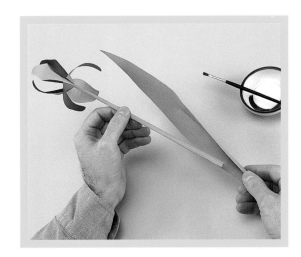

8 The finished iris—ready for display.

Iris Shortcuts

To cut folding time in half, fold two petal sets at once by stacking two cutouts together. Make sure all the petals are lined up and hold the layers firmly together as you cut. Make all the creases sharp and clean. Pull the two papers apart just before curling and shaping the petals.

Iris Gallery

I rises and leaves in a basket. The iris is a plant that carries itself well in a simple, uncluttered arrangement. A good balance of leaves supports the composition. If you stand the flowers up in aquarium gravel, the arrangement is easier to modify.

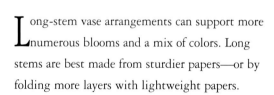

L ong-stem vase arrangements can support more numerous blooms and a mix of colors. Long stems are best made from sturdier papers—or by folding more layers with lightweight papers.

Framed arrangements of irises and a paper butterfly make an elegant wall decoration. Choose a deep frame to emphasize the 3-D effect of the flowers.

Give gift packages oriental grace by wrapping them in handmade Japanese paper with iris ornaments.

To make your compositions dynamic, always use an odd number of blooms and keep them few in number.

Paper Daylily

Daylily trumpets look like graceful butterflies that have landed on green stems.
Although their blooms last only a day in the garden, the paper variety keeps well
indoors. Thanks to hybrid flower breeders, there are many variations on the trumpet
shape of the daylily: some have wide, overlapping petals, some frilled, crinkled, and
ruffled petals, some are shaped like cups, others like small bells. In nature, daylily
colors range from pale lemon through soft tones of ivory to golden and apricot hues;
and from rose-pink, through delicate baby pink and violet, to deep burgundy,
maroon, and even purple.

Real daylilies are edible, paper daylilies are naturals as pretty garnishes for
desserts, formal place settings, or summer luncheon tables.

Materials

- *Daylily paper elements*

- *Scissors and/or X-acto knife*

- *White glue*

- *Ruler or other straightedge*

- *Scoring tool*

- *Toothpick*

How to Build a Daylily

Daylilies often grow wild along the edges of fields and roadways. Their short-lived blossoms are daily replaced by the successive bloom of abundant buds, which provides a long-lasting summer display. The main difference between daylilies and cultivated lilies is the appearance of their leaves; daylilies have long, grass-like leaves extending from the base of the plant. Easter and other cultivated lilies have short leaves that collar the stem.

The paper daylily method shown here is a simple way to get these showy blooms without having to water. Use them to quickly fill out a large flower arrangement. Life-size versions are also excellent for stage or window dressing. The simple leaf shape is easy to make in quantity by stacking together several layers of green paper and cutting freehand. Use the leaves by themselves to fill in and support arrangements of other long-stemmed flowers.

The daylily pattern is an especially good one to use on paper-backed fabrics. To create your own paper-backed fabric, choose a lightweight, small print gingham or calico fabric and apply a light coating of spray adhesive to the back. Next, press a sheet of colored tissue or other lightweight paper against the adhesive side of the fabric. Cut out the flower patterns from this material and create floral displays coordinated with the room interiors of your home.

Daylily Tips

- *For best effect, use two-tone paper with a light and dark hue of the same color. Use bright or dusty greens for the stems and leaves.*
- *Make long stems from heavyweight papers or extra folded-layers to keep them sturdy. Florist's wire is also useful.*
- *When using the lily as the only flower in an arrangement, cut stems to vary the length. Use lily leaves by themselves, as a graceful green accent in mixed paper flower arrangements.*

1 Score the center of three petals, along the three printed lines. These are the centerlines.

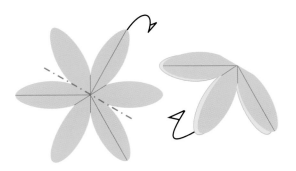

2 On the outside (light hue side) of the paper, mountain-fold and unfold across gap notches (between petals). Repeat with the other two sets of opposing gap notches. Fold the shape in half three times in this manner, then pierce the center to make a small hole for the stem.

3 On either side of the three centerlines is a mountain-crease. Fold each mountain-crease against and aligned to its corresponding centerline. Repeat with the other two sets of centerlines and mountain-folds. You will end up with three petals on the outside and three petals on the inside.

4 Glue together the overlapping paper of the outside petals, to keep the lily's trumpet shape tight. Let dry. Curl down the outside petals. Make some lilies more open than others. You may also have a few with the petals uncurled.

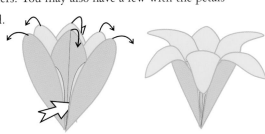

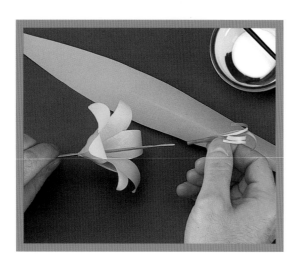

5 To make the filaments for the center, cut the provided paper into thin strips that remain connected at the bottom (see the indicated margin) (a). Curl this paper into a tight cylinder by wrapping it around a toothpick (b & c). Fan out the filaments and give each a slight curl (d).

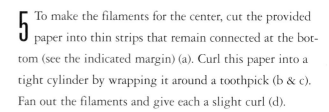

6 Make stems by folding stem paper in half twice, lengthwise, to make a thin, four-layered paper spear. Two-thirds from the bottom of the leaf, fold the leaf in half lengthwise. You may then leave the leaf straight or gently curl it downward.

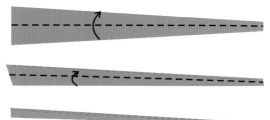

7 Insert the stem through the center hole from the bottom. Spear the cylinder end of the filament bundle with the protruding point of the stem, inside the trumpet of the flower. Use glue to keep the assembly secure.

8 Glue the leaf to the base of the stem. More than one leaf per stem and flower is a nice touch.

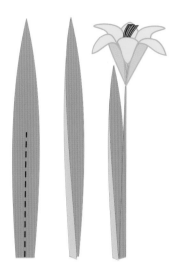

9 The finished daylily—ready for display.

Daylily Shortcuts

You can make long stems quickly by folding paper in half lengthwise, then cutting the folded edge of the paper away as a long and tapered stem shape. This stem paper will already be folded in half the long way. Also, try folding several layers of lightweight paper together and cutting out several stems at once.

Daylily Gallery

A paper butterfly lights on an arrangement of daylilies. The butterfly may be attached to a thin wire or glued directly to one of the blooms.

Daylily made of paper-backed fabric. Choose a light-weight fabric and attach a thin but strong backing paper with spray adhesive or paste. You can coordinate arrangements with any room or occasion.

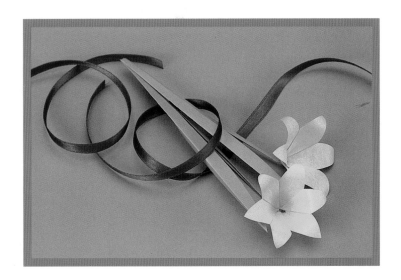

Miniature lilies make elegant gift ties. Gifts may be simply enclosed in a cloth or paper sack and decorated with a gift tie attached with ribbon.

Miniature daylilies make an attractive lapel pin. Glue the lily to a small clasp pin or attach it directly to your lapel with a straight pin.

Daylilies made of handmade Japanese papers. A long-stem arrangement in a tall vase is a quick and simple way to make a large accent piece. Notice that paper leaves are used as the support media, and show through the glass vase in an attractive way.

Paper Posies

Posies are small wildflowers, such as buttercups, that bloom in the late spring and summer. Lady-smock and cuckoo-flower are traditional names for posies. Fields of posies growing wild are a sign of high summer in England. Common to grassy slopes, and growing in hues of silver-white, delicate pink, and rich yellow, posies—whether paper or perennial—look best arranged together in small vases, or in a small nosegay, tied-up with a ribbon. Without scent, but sweet in their appearance, posies suggest innocence and informality. Paper with a subtle sheen is best to reflect the silky, slightly waxy quality of posy flower petals.

How to Build a Posy

osies can be a single, small, fragrant flower or a bunch of them. Posy is the informal name for wildflowers, gathered during a pleasant stroll and assembled into a spontaneous bouquet.

The posy selection here contains two types of small flowers: daisies and buttercups. Each is quick and easy to make—you can fill a May basket in no time. Do not hesitate to add these little paper flowers to any dried flower arrangement; they will fit in quite nicely.

Some paper butterflies are also included, to add to the effect of a bright, summer afternoon. You may wish to create your own butterflies by painting butterfly wing patterns on watercolor paper and using the cut-and-fold method as indicated on the pattern sheet.

Materials

- *Posy paper elements*

- *Scissors*

- *White glue*

- *Ruler or other straightedge*

- *Scoring tool*

- *Pencil (to open a hole in the base of the blossom)*

- *Toothpick*

Posy Tips

- *Choose colors typical of wildflowers, especially violet, yellow and white. Use drab or deep greens for the stems, to reflect that these are summer plants.*

- *The two-tone paper supplied for this project has a different color on each side. You can fold the project with either side outward.*

- *Add leaves from the other flower patterns in this book. Glue the leaves and blossoms in place for permanence.*

- *Tie together a bouquet of posies with ribbon and lace for a formal occasion or string them together to make garlands and leis.*

- *Cut butterfly shapes out of any brightly colored or patterned papers. Butterflies make great accents to any arrangement. Use them to decorate packages or as a brooch.*

To Make a Buttercup

1 Following the lines indicated, score one side of the paper buttercup pattern. This will be the "show side". You may lightly pencil these lines in first if you are not sure you are clear on their arrangement. Turn paper over.

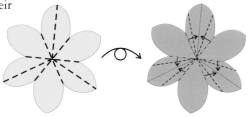

2 Fold the short creases (located between each petal) to touch and align with the long creases (running through the center of three of the petals). Notice that there are only three long creases and each long crease has a short crease on either side. If you fold correctly, the finished piece will look like an upside-down, conical paper cup. Turn the form over.

3 From this view you can see inside the buttercup—the three narrow petals will be very distinct. Using a pencil or toothpick, pierce a hole in the center. Do not make this hole too large—leave the paper snug enough for the stem to get a good hold.

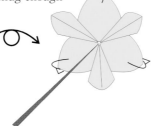

4 Make stems by folding stem paper in half lengthwise, twice, to get a thin, four-layered paper spear.

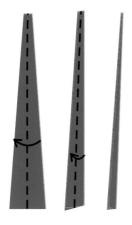

5 Insert the paper stem into the hole.

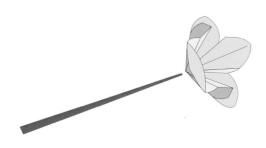

To Make a Daisy

6 Score or valley-fold creases up the center of each petal. Make sure that these folds are neat and crisp. Turn paper over. Score or valley-crease folds running straight between each petal. Again, be neat and crisp. Using a pencil or toothpick, pierce a hole in the center. Do not make this hole too large—leave the paper snug enough for the stem to get a good hold. Push stem paper through the center hole from the underside, working until the fit is very snug. Either side of the paper will work for the outside of the flower. You may also add the button center described in the Daisy project. Trim any excess stem paper from the flowerleaf center.

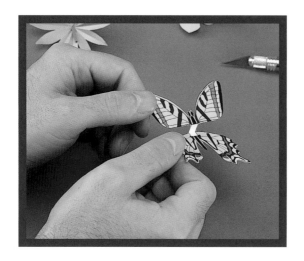

To Make a Butterfly

7 Mountain and valley-fold, as indicated in the diagrams, to bring the forewings to the hindwings (a). The forewings should overlap the hindwings slightly (as they do in real butterflies). Mountain-fold the center of the butterfly's body. Valley-fold along the body and wing attachment lines to bring the wings into a natural position (b).

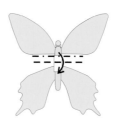

8 The finished butterfly. Add a butterfly or two to any summer bouquet of flowers.

9 Cut out the paper vase elements in the back pocket of this book and valley-fold on the dashed lines. Paste tab (a) to inner edge (b) and tab (c) to inner edge (d). Place the completed vase over a small can or plastic drinking cup and fill with paper flowers.

10 The completed project: paper vase, posies, and butterfly.

Posy Shortcuts

Save time cutting out flowerleaf elements by stacking up four sheets of colored paper and cutting them all at once. Trace the outline of the template onto the top layer of the paper stack, then cut. Be sure to keep all of the paper layers tightly together as you cut.

Posy Gallery

Coffee cake garnished with daisy and buttercup blossoms. Use paper posies to garnish all types of salads and desserts.

A May basket filled with posies is a delightful project for young and old. The basket is a simple, construction paper cylinder wrapped around a paper cup. The edges of the basket were made fancy with scissor-cut fringe. A long strip of construction paper makes a good handle.

Posies arranged in a simple pitcher. A cheerful accent piece or gift. Make longer stems and create colorful arrangements in any container.

String together buttercup blossoms to make a lei or garland to grace an item or a setting. A needle and thread make quick work of this lovely floral accent piece.

A gathering of paper posies makes a fine nosegay. A ten-inch piece of green paper cut and folded in a buttercup pattern serves as collar and background to this hand-held arrangement.

Paper Lotus

How to Build a Lotus

Exotic and mysterious are the words traditionally used to describe the lotus or water lily. Lotus blossoms set against the dark and quiet water of a secluded pond are one of nature's most evocative and enchanting displays.

Although it appears complex, the lotus that follows is one of the easiest constructions in the book. It is also the most beautiful. You will be surprised at how effectively a single lotus blossom and lily pad can cast splendid spell. Arrangements of water lilies are perfect for dinner table centerpieces, the coffee table, or a display shelf in the book case. You can use your most elegant papers on this model. However, even plain white shelf paper will be transformed when you fold it into a lotus. Scale the pattern as large or as small as needed for your arrangement—or make the flowers more lush by adding extra layers of paper.

Materials

- *Lotus paper elements*
- *Scissors*
- *White glue*
- *Ruler or other straightedge*
- *Scoring tool*
- *Pencil*

Lotus Tips

- *Any color is suitable for the blossom, in nature lotus colors range from deep crimson to stark white.*
- *To float paper lotus blossoms, make thin wax floats by dripping melted wax onto a cold water surface. Place the floats on the surface of a punch bowl or beverage and rest the lotus blossoms on top.*
- *Use only food-grade waxed papers for lotuses to garnish food. Glue the flower elements together with drops of melted candle wax instead of paste or glue.*
- *Always use caution when working with melted wax and flame. Keep any candle flame away from paper ornaments.*

1 Score or valley-fold the center of each petal. Do this to all three pink sets of petals and both yellow sets. It does not matter which side of the paper you choose, so long as all the creases are valley-folds. The valley-fold side will be the inner side of the finished flower.

2 Valley-fold along the base of each petal. Do this to all three pink sets of petals and both yellow sets.

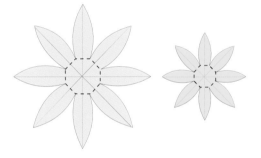

3 Apply a little glue or paste to the center of the underside (mountain-fold side) of each element and stack them one on top of the other as shown in the diagram. Be sure to rotate each petal set so that the petals from one layer show between the petals above it. Press together firmly and let dry. The petals in the center should be more tightly closed than outer petals.

4 Put a valley-crease through the middle of the lily pad. This will be the outer side of the leaf.

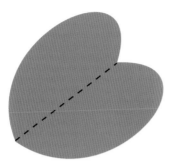

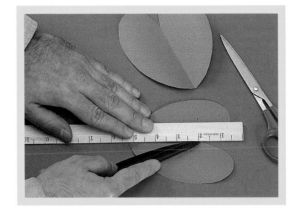

5 You may curl the outer edges of the leaves up or down for a more natural effect.

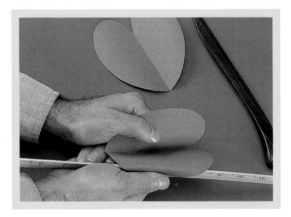

6 The completed lotus—ready for display.

Lotus Shortcuts

When making lotus from tissue paper or baking parchment, stack up to six layers of paper for each shape cutout. Trace the template on the top layer of the stack and cut all six layers at once. You can also fold up to three layers at a time.

Lotus Gallery

A lotus and paper frog in a display setting. (The frog project is featured in *Paper Animals*, book three in this series.)

Make a decorative indoor wreath of lotus and rose elements. Alternate color layers of lotus elements to support and frame each rose blossom. Secure each piece to a cardboard ring and a loop of cord attached to the back for hanging. A hot-melt glue gun makes quick work of the final assembly.

To beautify a formal dinner setting, use a paper lotus to fill each guest's empty plate. Each guest can then keep their lotus as a memento.

Float a lotus bloom in a punch bowl for an exotic touch. Make the blossom out of waxed paper or foil and set it on top of a wax float that is at least the diameter of the base of the bloom. Remove from bowl at serving time.

The lotus makes a wonderful table centerpiece because of its elegance and low height. You can also make blossoms to match your dinner napkins. Back fabric pieces with paper to make them suitably foldable. Practice on scrap material first.

Paper Cactus

How to Build a Cactus

The flowering cactus is romantic: One is reminded of painted deserts, western sunsets, and the lone cry of the coyote. The beautiful blossoming of an otherwise drab and humble plant is a Cinderella story, illustrative of hope and self-confidence. The cactus is all this and more.

Our cactus is a simple construction; easily modified and quick to assemble, you can arrange a tabletop desert in no time. Create cacti to accent a summer dinner party or to adorn gifts. Or present one to friends who have trouble keeping potted plants alive. Although these paper models look realistic, they are best kept from water completely.

Finally, be creative with the choice of materials and dimensions of the cacti you make on your own. Use paper-backed fabrics or vinyl wallpapers for their durability and texture. And the size of these materials will allow you to construct some very large specimens indeed, as you will see in the showcase section of this chapter.

Materials

- *Cactus paper elements*

- *Scissors*

- *White glue*

- *Ruler or other straightedge*

- *Scoring tool*

- *Pencil*

- *Flower pot, tray or planter*

- *Aquarium gravel or sand*

Cactus Tips

- *Choose rich green colors in glossy or semi-glossy materials. The cactus plant is a succulent; the material should look appetizing. Any color paper is suitable for the blossom.*
- *Make small cactus shapes and attach to large cacti as buds. Blossom and bud elements should be glued in place for permanence.*
- *Display finished cacti with sand or terra-cotta colors. Natural materials are especially effective. Fill a tray or planter with aquarium gravel or sand for an easy "anchor" medium.*
- *Vary the number and proportions of the radial arms of the cactus plant pattern to create cacti of all shapes and sizes.*

Paper Flowers

1 Score or valley-fold the center of each petal, and the area between each petal. Turn the paper over.

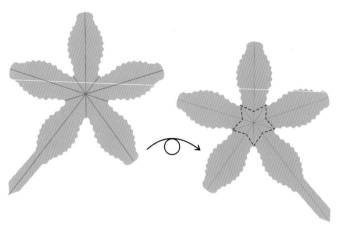

2 Score a five pointed star (dotted lines provided) on the inside surface of the model paper. Use a pencil for this step, since the pencil marks will not be visible once the model is folded.

Glue at white areas

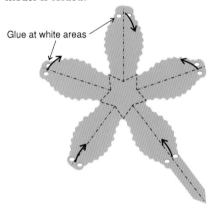

3 Apply glue or paste to the ends of the inside paper surfaces (side of paper with the star). Mountain- and valley-fold on the crease lines to close and shape the cactus plant. Hold surfaces together until the glue sets.

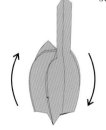

4 Rotate the model so that the anchoring spike points down. Create a cactus blossom from the provided material, following the folding and construction method for the buttercup in the posy instruction set. Insert the stem of the completed blossom between paper layers of the cactus plant so that the blossom is seated firmly and attractively.

5 Plant the paper spike into the selected medium. It is not necessary to have a blossom on each cactus if more than one plant is displayed in the same arrangement.

6 The finished cactus plant—ready for display.

Cactus Shortcuts

Try free-folding the cactus shape, without scoring or pre-creasing, and apply only a light pressure on the folds to make a softer form. This is especially good for cacti folded from soft papers and paper-backed fabric.

Cactus Gallery

The cactus makes an unusual package ornament. Wrap the package first, then make a small slit through the wrapping paper wherever you want to place a cactus. Flatten the pointed planting tab and slip it into the slot in the wrap. Crease the base of the tab firmly, so the cactus will stand upright.

You can modify the basic cactus pattern proportions to create cacti of all sizes and dimensions. Make small cacti and attach as budding nodules, with or without blossoms.

A festive buffet setting. The cactus pictured is made of paper-backed fabric and the tortilla chips are handmade paper. The cactus coordinates with the cloth dinner napkins. Choose a light-weight fabric and apply a thin but strong backing paper with spray adhesive or paste.

Arrange cacti on fabric, paper or sand for a background or display. Add some natural materials for texture and effect—scale from miniature to life-size.

Arrangements of cacti in terra-cotta pots look very realistic. Mix and match blossom colors, you can even use different textures and shades of green among the cacti plants themselves. Fill pots with sand or gravel for easy "planting."

About the Author

Michael G. LaFosse has been designing, creating, and teaching origami for more than twenty years. Inspired when he was just twelve by the work of origami master Akira Yoshizawa, LaFosse began making and folding paper to create his own origami designs. Often sculptural, his work is not always immediately recognizable as origami. However, most pieces originate from a single square of uncut paper. Favorite subjects for LaFosse's origami are taken from nature: flowers and animals that he studies in their natural habitats. He often makes his own paper for these designs, imagining the paper as the "flesh" and the folds as the "bones", striving to create lifelike origami with all the character and attitude of the original subject.

How is it possible to convey nature's poetry and spirit within the folds of a single piece of paper? LaFosse's exquisite work shows that paper folding is a three-dimensional drawing process, and an art in and of itself.

Acknowledgements

I am grateful to Rockport Publishers for allowing me to participate in their paper craft series, and for their encouragement and enthusiasm throughout. I especially wish to thank the following people for lending their talent and courteous help in the production of this book: Casandra McIntyre and the people at Rugg Road Papers, Boston, Massachusetts, for bringing my work to the publisher's attention, and for their continued support of the paper arts community at large. Shawna Mullen for reviewing, editing, and refining the manuscript. Winnie Danenbarger and Barbara States for shaping the series concept and making timely suggestions along the way. Rosalie Grattaroti for her enthusiasm in taking care of the many details that connect author and publisher. Douglas Cannon for his photographic work and advice during the concept stages of production. Michael Lafferty for his patient work on the "how to" and showcase photography. Ashley Wyatt for set direction during the step-by-step photography. Lynne Havighurst for her artistic direction and for bringing the many elements together beautifully.

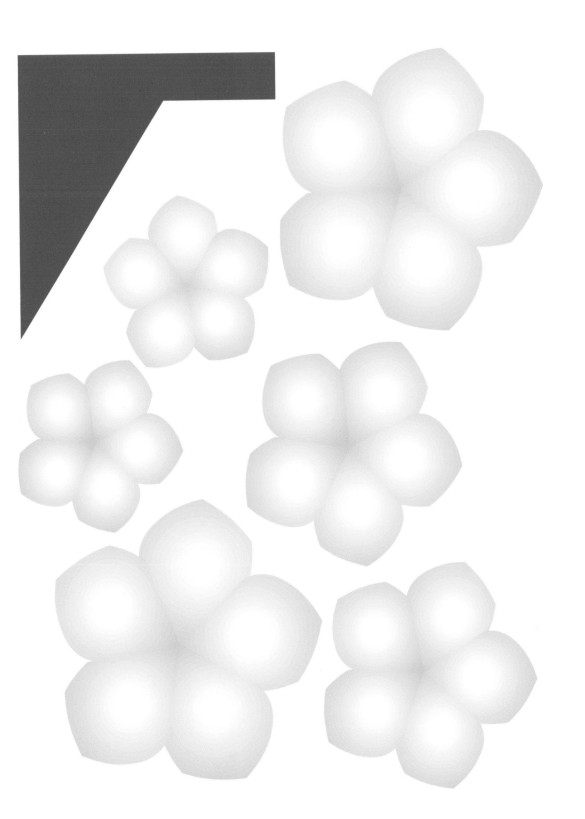

Rose Paper Elements – 2 of 2

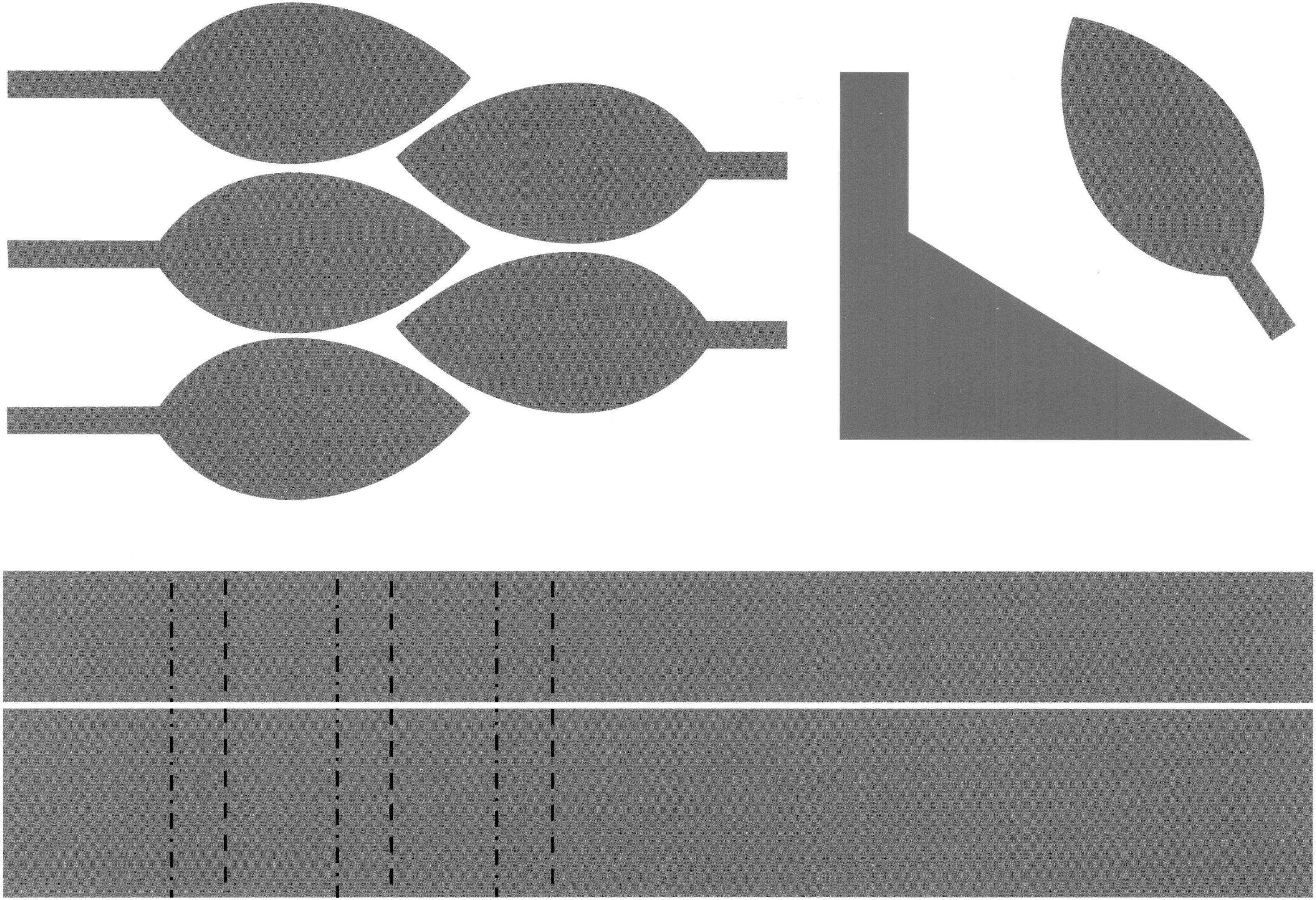

Tulip Paper Elements – 1 of 2
To make two tulips

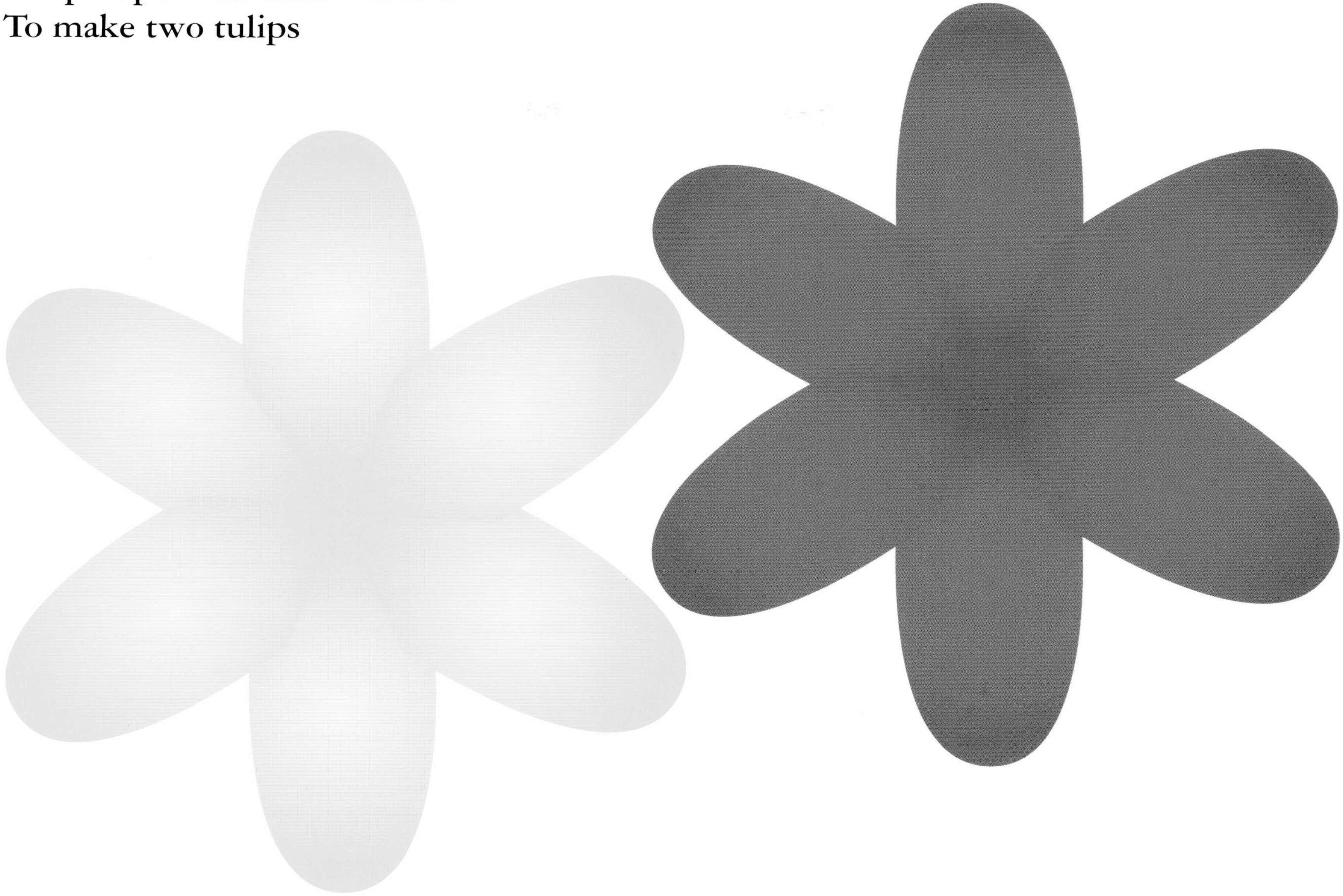

Iris Paper Elements – 1 of 2
To make two irises

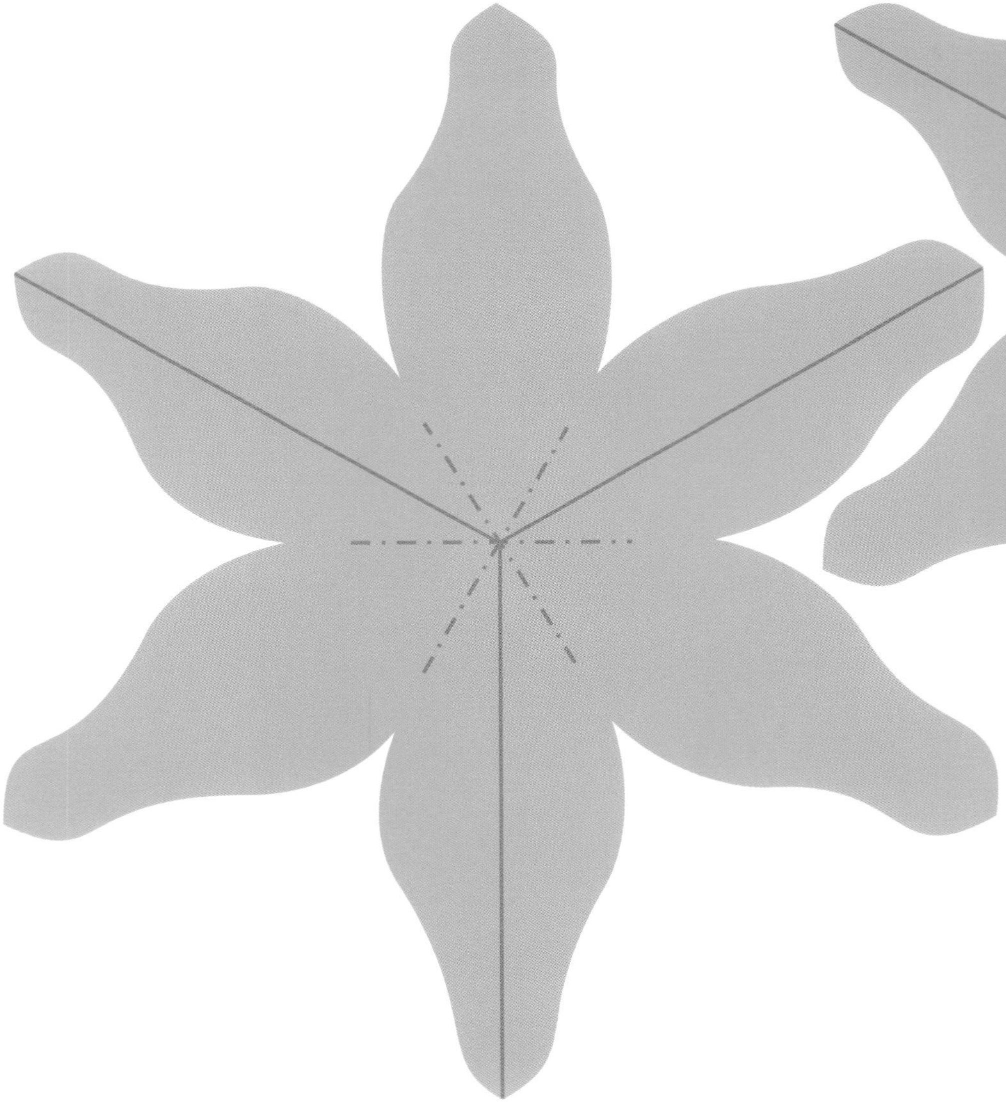

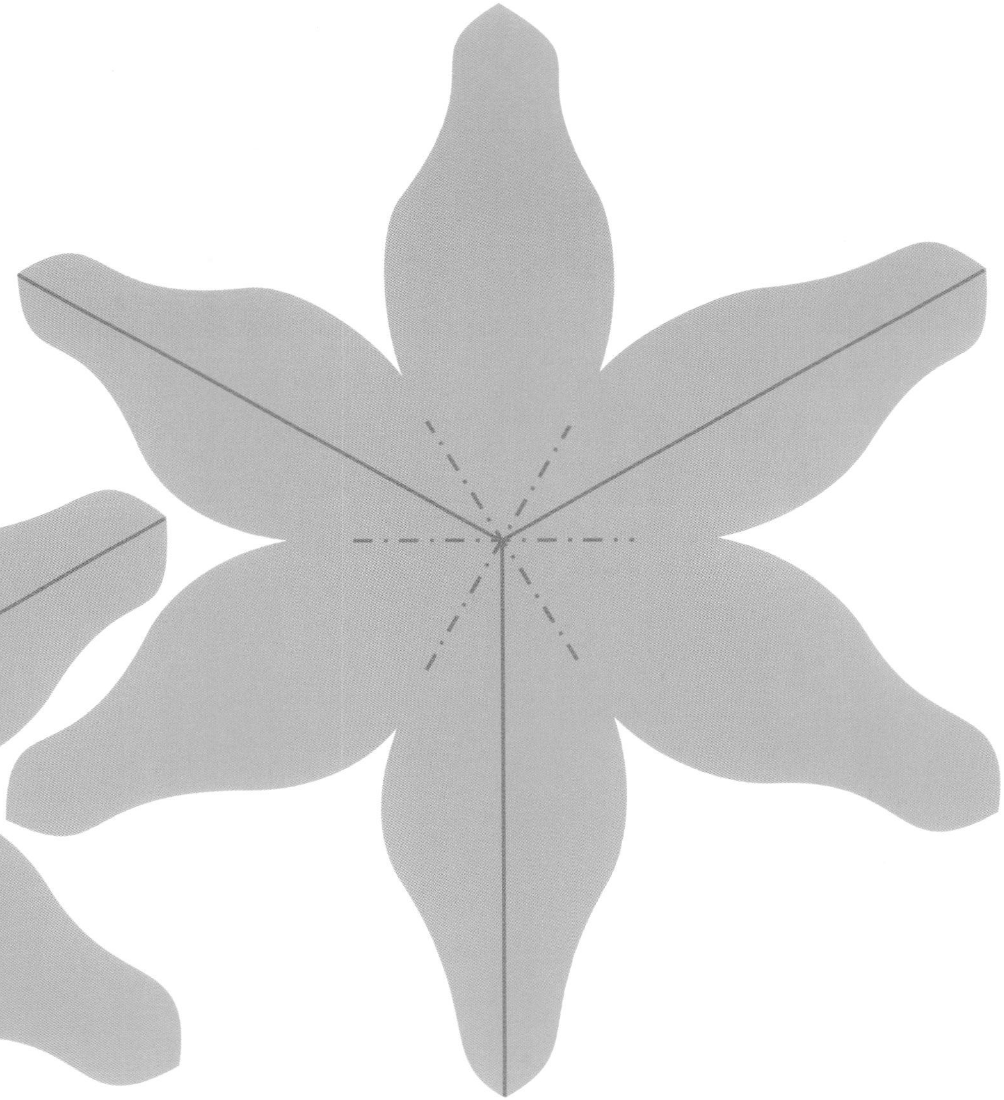

Daylily Paper Elements – 1 of 2
To make two daylilies

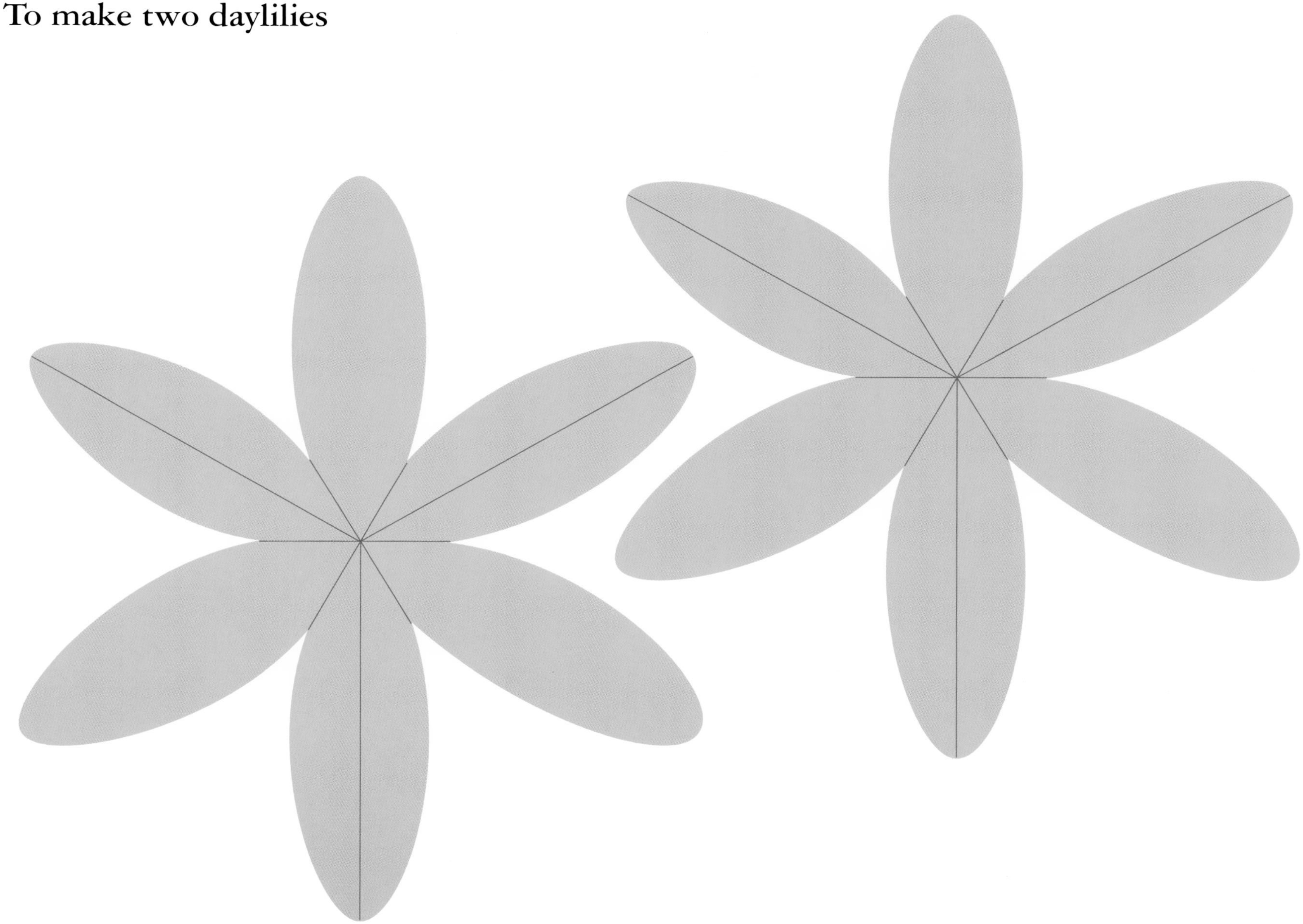

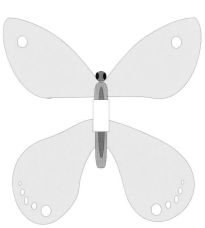
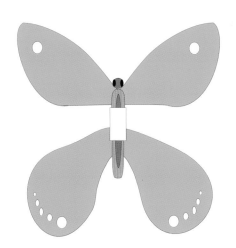
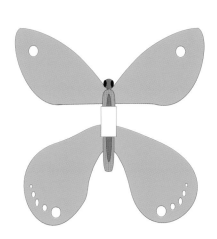

Posy Paper Elements – 3 of 3

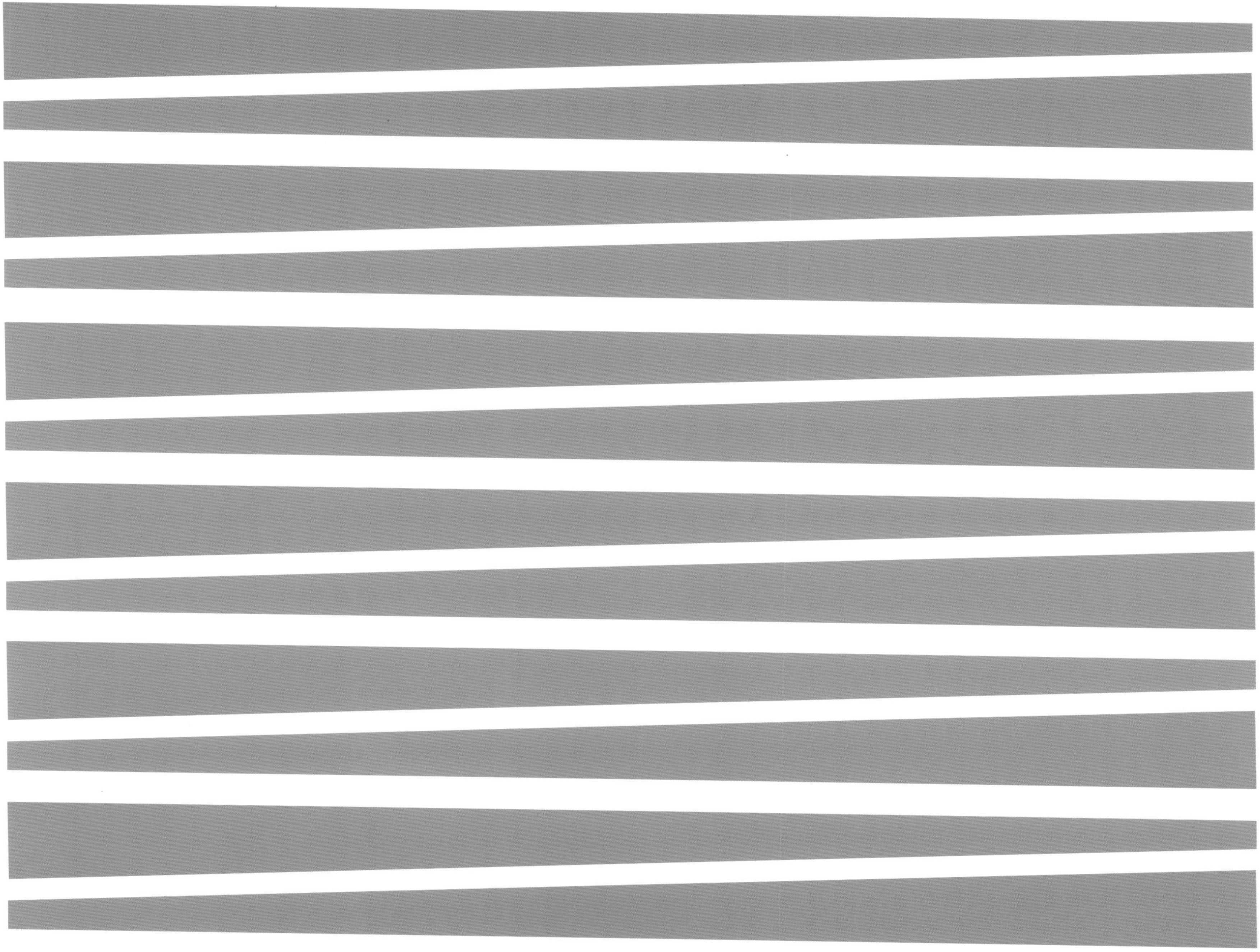

Cactus Paper Elements – 1 of 1

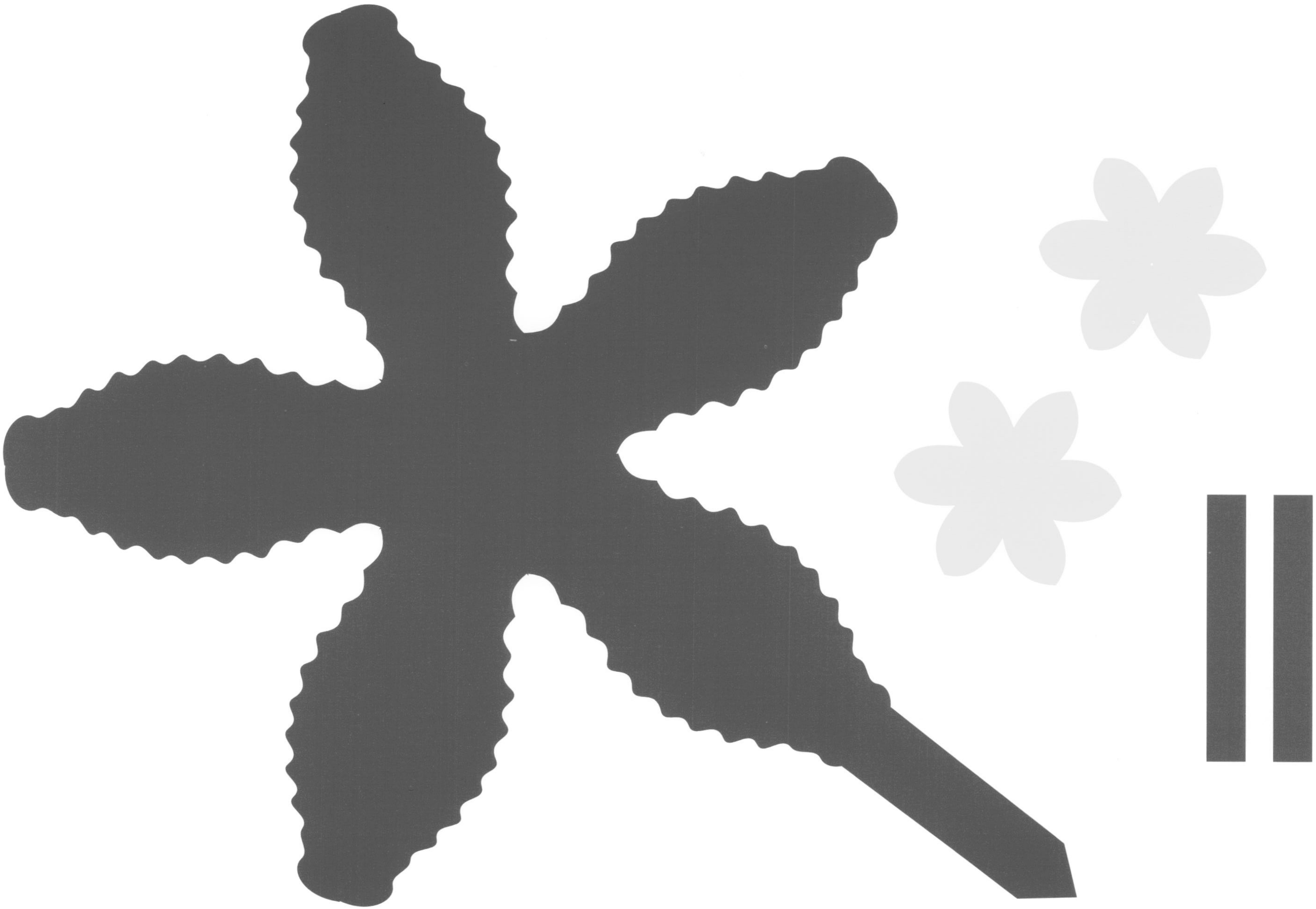

Lotus Paper Elements – 1 of 2

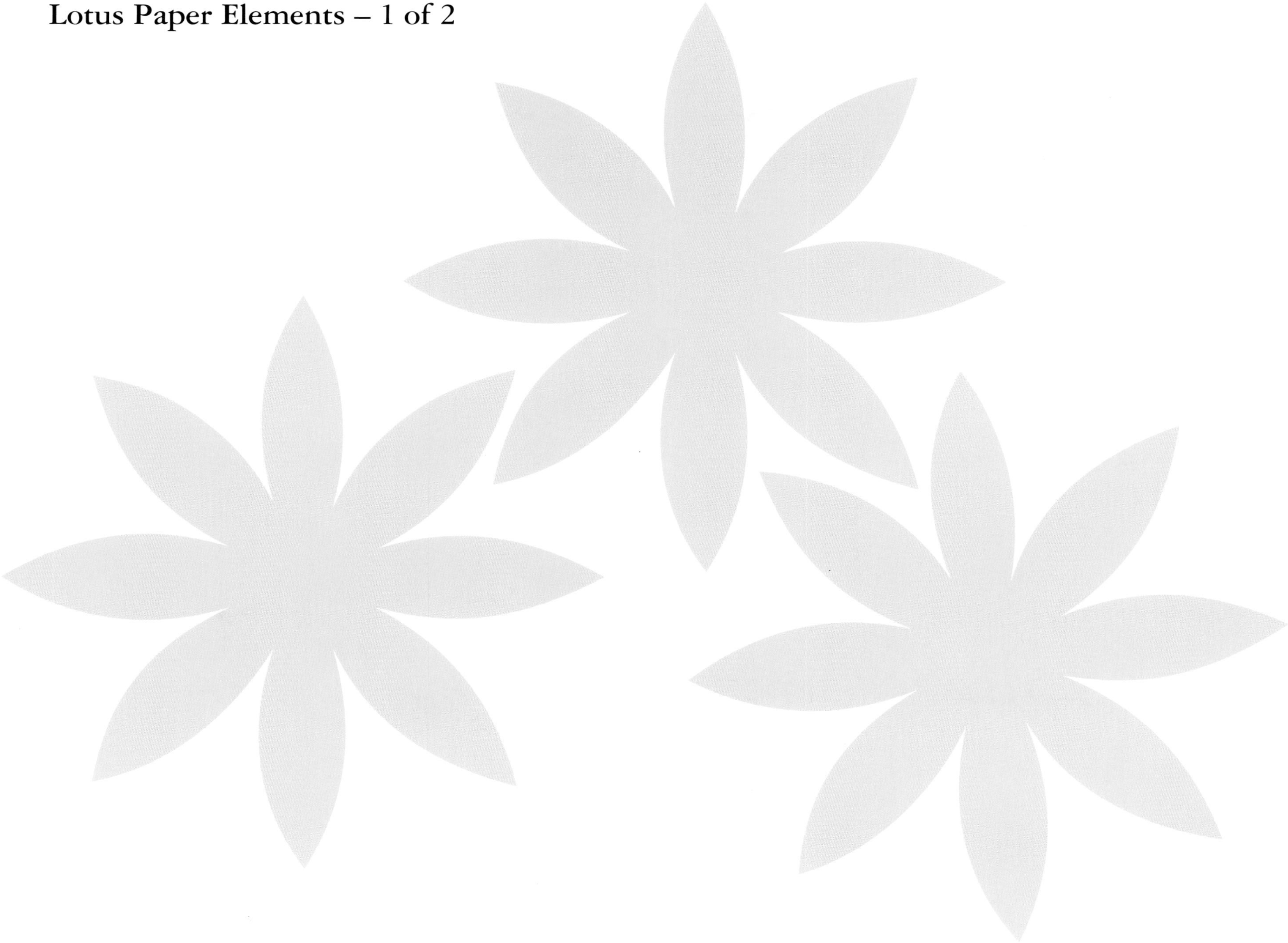

Lotus Paper Elements – 2 of 2

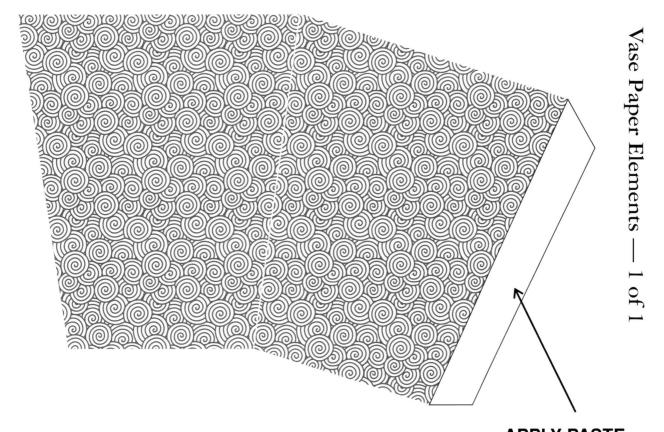

APPLY PASTE

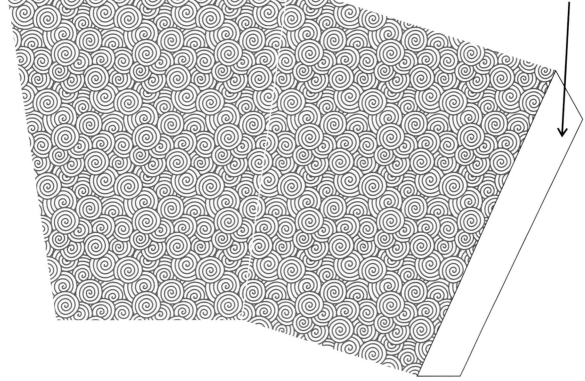

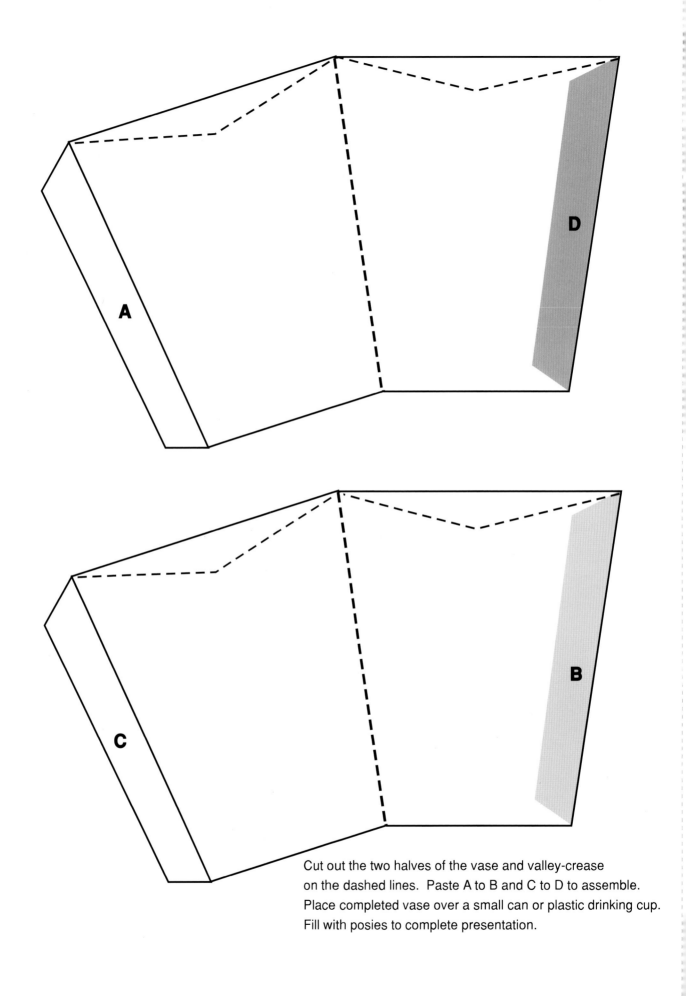

Cut out the two halves of the vase and valley-crease
on the dashed lines. Paste A to B and C to D to assemble.
Place completed vase over a small can or plastic drinking cup.
Fill with posies to complete presentation.

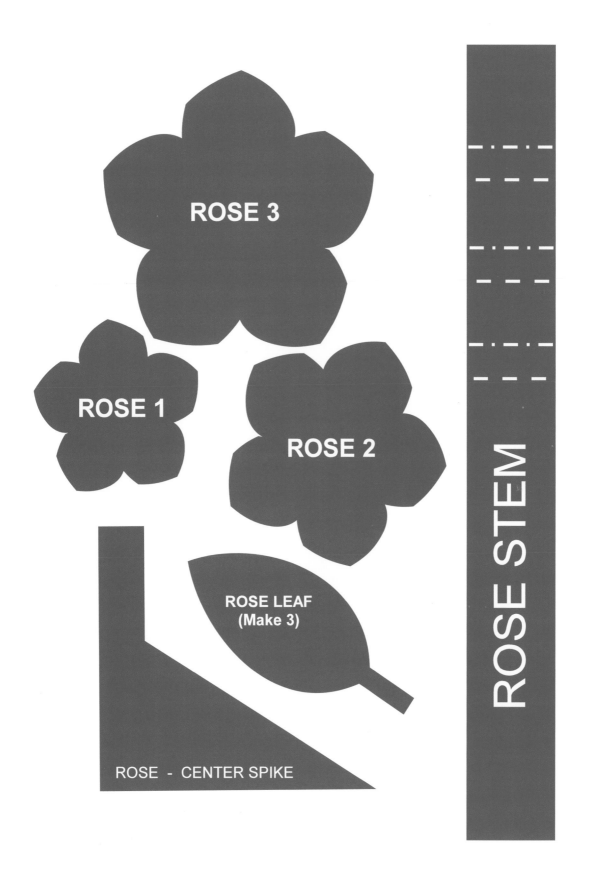

ROSE 3

ROSE 1

ROSE 2

ROSE LEAF
(Make 3)

ROSE - CENTER SPIKE

ROSE STEM

Rose Template

Tulip Template

TULIP FLOWER

TULIP 1/2 LEAF

TULIP STEM

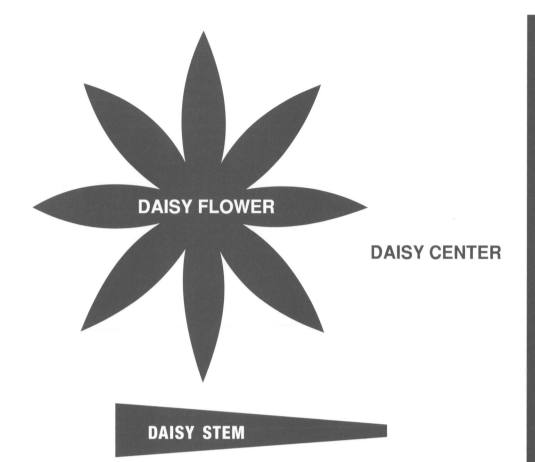

DAISY FLOWER

DAISY CENTER

Daisy Template

DAISY STEM

DAISY LEAF

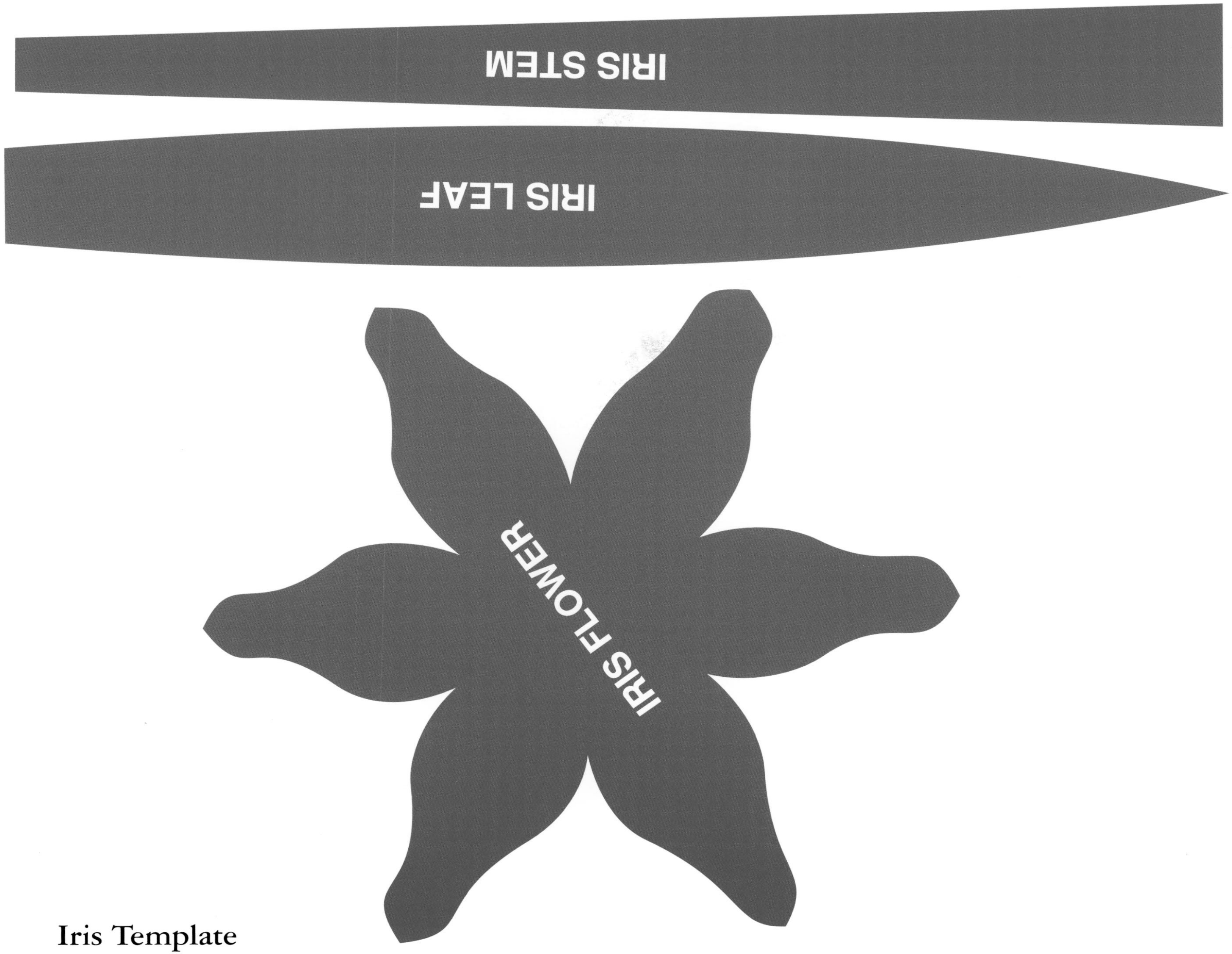

Iris Template

IRIS FLOWER

IRIS LEAF

IRIS STEM

Daylily Template

DAYLILY LEAF TOP

DAYLILY LEAF BOTTOM

DAYLILY FLOWER

DAYLILY STEM TOP

DAYLILY STEM BOTTOM

Posy Template

POSY
DAISY

POSY
CUP

SULPHUR
BUTTERFLY

POSY STEM

SWALLOWTAIL
BUTTERFLY

LOTUS
PETALS

LOTUS
CENTER

LILY PAD

CACTUS

CACTUS FLOWER STEM

CACTUS FLOWER

Vase Template